Little Thistles

Winner of the
2023 New Women's Voices Series

poems by

Stacey R. Forbes

Finishing Line Press
Georgetown, Kentucky

Little Thistles

New Women's Voices Series, No. 178

ACKNOWLEDGMENTS

My gratitude to the editors who published the following poems in their
journals:

Atlanta Review: "And did we love"
Barren: "For my mother, walking in the woods at night
on the anniversary of my father's death" and "Strata"
Beloit Poetry Journal: "All we have left"
Blue Mountain Review: "Cake"
Crab Creek Review: "Dream with mother of pearl"
Haunted Waters Press: "When I am wild with grief, the animal in me"
Split Rock Review: "Flying north, a war story"
Terrain.org: "No greater love," "Call and response," "Signs," and "Streams"

Publisher: Leah Huete de Maines
Editor: Christen Kincaid
Cover Art: *Desert Thistle* by Michele Marie Miller ©2023
Author Photo: Ryan Mihalyi
Cover Design: Elizabeth Maines McCleavy

Order online: www.finishinglinepress.com
also available on amazon.com

Author inquiries and mail orders:
Finishing Line Press
PO Box 1626
Georgetown, Kentucky 40324
USA

Contents

With gratitude to my mother, who will always be an oak.
To Michele, Barbara and Steven, who made this book possible.
And to Dr. Tom Grogan, who said, "Stick with the sting.
It's where the story is."

Feather, body, bone

Still as stone, I watch
a bird pluck another
bird from the air, light
in a tree and eat her—
such small wings to cross
the miles of Mexican
poppies—fractured
feathers fall like snow
to sanctify the barren
ground behind this house.
How many times have
I prayed for the body
in motion? The body
at rest doesn't know
that it's already dead.
The owl swallows
the heart of the red finch,
her lungs, swollen
with song, and carries
them back to the sky.
Later, he casts out the
skeleton's long quills.
The claws that held on.
What lives in light
does not disappear
in an hour, an autumn,
whole winters of hunger
that wait in the trees.
This breathless, bewildering
desert is God's body.
Even the cactus has bones.

Call and response

I called to say I saw lightning. I wanted to know if you needed cream to cloud your coffee in the morning. It's too early for summer storms, but the desert is ready to whet the whistle of the fledgling hawk, fallen from its nest. Did you remember to bring in the cat? The coyote's song always ends on the same note. I left a note on the freezer for you. Open the door, cool your face for a moment. Count the fins on the steelhead trout. Do we ever have enough? Remember when we got our fish from the Shoshone-Bannock dragging coolers like life rafts down the west bank of the river? Did you hear the lake is now so low you can hit rock bottom without even trying? I saw the news in the checkout line. No one counted on so many bones, murdered bodies among the tadpoles small enough to live in such shallows. The half-tame javelina in our backyard ate our last three peaches and left their hard hearts on our porch. Do you believe in omens? I called to warn you about the speed trap between the two saguaros on the road home. I called to ask what I could bring that would make any difference. I called to ask how hungry you are. To see if you needed my hands to brush your hair from your eyes. If you recognize my number, even in this heat. I wanted to say that I have always thought of you as cool. That I'm lost. That all I can do is drive. That I love you. That I already know you won't answer.

All we have left

That summer, our laughter spread
like chokeberries over the ground,

foxes and rock squirrels barking
beneath: come. It's getting dark.

I had never known a woman like you,
hair like a nest of golden flickers,

white blouse missing buttons and
never clean, your breastbone grazed

by red wine and paint. By the blood
of a spotted fawn you found

on the road and photographed.
After, you gave her to the ground

and a God you don't believe in
cradled her body in frost.

Did we ever sleep in such peace?
Your house haunts me even now

with its relics—sainted snakes and
rabbits, your mother's cracked china,

heart of Mary blazing as we looted
your grown-over yard for lemons.

I never spent the night. You told me
about the scorpions in your shower.

How you finished a wounded mouse
the cat left in your kitchen with a shovel.

I wasn't strong enough for the kind
of mercy your life required. What's more,

I couldn't close your bathroom door
because the tulip you painted—

bigger than both of us—was wedged there.
The walls would not bear the weight

of another framed, once-living thing.
Nothing you loved has ever escaped

your nails. My heart was clumsy.
A fall was inevitable.

I brought the wrong gift: wild onion
bulbs in plastic cups. You cried

because everything was dying
and I was too happy to see it.

Your fury was beautiful.
You were the earth.

In the end, you refused paper napkins.
Said the holiness of trees is all we have

left. Goodbye was the last of your
limoncello, straight from the jar.

We sat in the dark and drank till
the world dripped from our chins.

Strata

—Excerpts from an Arizona orchard

1

Six days into spring and I am sitting in the kitchen
tending tins of dirt in the oven. Two hundred
and twenty degrees Fahrenheit bakes the last of the
rain from the soil we took from the orchard.
Our experiment asks: how much water is gone,
and how long can we live with what's left?
I'm falling in love with the warm earth. I want to sift it
like a powdered sugar into my father's fresh grave.
I want to fashion a blanket for him from strata gathered
with care and cradled for days in banana bread tins.
Sweetness we never knew how to give to the living.

2

There is much to be discovered.
I don't cry, but sometimes hives appear
above my heart. I fall asleep dreaming
of bees, carrying our memories
from tree to tree, humming love, bearing
more fruit than our thin limbs can hold.

3

We long for the nectar.
We live with the sting.

4

Out of the oven, the earth is sometimes
powder, sometimes clay, always on the verge
of crumbling. We bake away more water.
How carefully we measure what is lost.

5

We are not stars; we are the offspring
of organic hearts—salt of the earth, old
as dirt. Seeds in search of fertile ground.

6
Back in the field, our lungs fill with light.
We want to be essential as the earthworm
that breathes through its skin.

7
One day, my father will come up for air.
He will be trees, peaches, pistachios,
drinking from the mouths of bees.

8
And so we sit with incubators in our kitchen.
We learn from dirt how to hold rain for days,
no matter the heat, or the darkness.
We document the weight, the density
of our desire to drink our fill. We teach
the orchard keepers what is needed—
when to flood the fields and when
to say, enough. We sanctify our hands
to hold the sacred rite of watering our fathers.

Streams
—For Gabriel, age nine

The angel Gabriel wanted to pee in the stream. He asked his mother, reverent up to her shins in minnows. Her pink bikini was sweet as salvation. The only thing sweeter was Gabriel's face, father-forsaken and beautiful under his crooked cap. Hopping on slippery rocks, he did the only dance the call of nature knows. His mother's eyes were mangers, soft and dark. Please, she said. Just pee downstream. We bob in the water, wondering how the canyon was carved. How many tadpoles wish for our long legs, kicking in clear water. If turtles will snap at our strawberry toes. We know the rattlesnakes are mating, that leopard frogs are spilling eggs like stars into the milky way of animal attraction, that cicadas wait seventeen years underground to crawl into the light and sing for their mates only once. That there will be no buzz like love. That we are capable of killing or curing each other. That long ago a glacier pierced this place and water gushed from its side. That another storm is coming. That children, still native to joy in spite of us, believe what springs inside them is clean. For once in our lives, we won't run away. We are ready to rise with the flood.

The lightning field

It will make you gasp. It might
make you want to stay alive, even.
—Ross Gay

The stillness in me breaks
into rain and I am

suddenly, incurably
alive. A deluge of love

for this desert is wrung
from my body in drops—

cumulonimbus   creosote

      hatchling   howl

owl's clover   tempest

        timbre

  coati   catclaw acacia   sombras

      night-bloom

alluvion   downpour and

     drench

Soaked to the bone, I press
into the arms of the storm.

I am el deseo, she who wants
to come close. Lightning

strikes and I become
what I have always been—

a clearing. A crescent.
A woman waxing to light.

Cake

And for my fifty-second birthday—bats
with a crush on my car, drawn from the dusk
by the drowsy bug hum of my engine.
Bob Dylan singing Tangled Up in Blue.
Sun falling asleep on a back road home
and me a little lost. White lights warming
a stranger's backyard and wild poppies
bowing their heads to sleep, or to pray
they will open their apricot hearts
one more time in the morning.
This is the kind of beautiful that hurts.
I drive slowly because I know
how fast this magic will go
somewhere I'll never find it again.
There is a cat named after the moon
who waits for me in the window
and still lights at the sight of me,
though we are both older now.
There is the steady gaze of a man,
warm and dark as a summer night's rain.
There is the sister-friend who hangs
old pictures on new walls for me,
no matter how many times I move.
There is love from a cousin
I thought I had lost long ago and
my mother's small voice on the phone,
her hair turning white as the birches
that surround her like a house
I haven't visited in years.
Birches like candles on a cake
that is smothered in somebody's love.
How does a life become such sweetness?
Soft as frosting, evening falls
as the sonar, the radio waves,
the voices I'm straining to hear
slice right through me.

Flying north, a war story

No one told the birds
in Arizona that Kiev is burning,
that soldiers ripped doors
from their hinges and blew out
the windows in somebody's
kitchen before the warm ball
of bread could rise. The sun
comes up in Tucson and the
mourning doves fill their bellies
with song.

The birds have fled St. Petersburg
and not returned because
they cannot carry this terrible
cold in their bones—only crows
and ravens remain on rooftops;
their cries are sniper fire—they are
always awake; they turn in the wind
to show us the weather.
They will never be known
for their music.

In love and oblivious,
an Arctic tern drops a fish
at the feet of his mate. How many
times will they fly to the Cape
of Good Hope only to see another
fledgling fall from the sky?
They know they can only feed
what holds the will to live.
Still, they stand together on the ice
with Argentina in their eyes.

The largest owl in the world
is endangered—fewer than four
hundred Blakiston's fish owls
living like whispers in Russia's

far east. Rumors of six-foot
wingspans reach as far as Ukraine,
where children lie quiet as mines
in their beds. Their mothers call
out in their sleep, guarding the dark
with the sounds of owls.

My mother nearly named me
Anastasia. So beautiful, she said,
though it's not our native tongue.
I never knew the fish owl's name
until today, or Yulia, the old woman
shot where she knelt in her squash
garden, clucking at roots still curled
in the earth. We are endangered.
In a dream, I fly north for the spring,
find the nest of a passenger pigeon.

I shield the small egg with my body.
I say, I'm sorry. Please come back.

No place like home

Memphis has been shaken by several killings, including the shooting of a pastor during a daylight carjacking in her driveway...and the slaying of a jogger abducted during her pre-dawn run... —NPR news, Sept. 8, 2022

My father's car tried to kill me tonight.
It was me at the wheel and no moon

when a thunderstorm slashed the hood
and choked the headlights.

Every ache on the radio stuck
in my throat: Walking in Memphis.

Running in Memphis. Kidnapped
and murdered in Memphis.

Stealing and shooting and bleeding
and wailing and sirens and singing

and I sang along: boy, you
got a prayer in Memphis

as the windshield wipers beat
their wings against the glass.

My father was born in Tennessee
and passed quietly in the fall.

Elvis was dead already.
They both died at home.

I bought my father's car from
my mother to keep him with me.

Sometimes his radio drives me head-on
into the acoustics of blues, the phantom

pain of touch, the sugar-in-flames taste
of bourbon, the smell of strong coffee

that calls in the morning and says,
come back. There's no place like home

to tear a heart in two.
Home is where the hawk is.

The harvest moon emerges
as I pull into the drive.

Outside my house is a tree
and under the tree, half a dove.

**For my mother, walking in the woods at night
on the anniversary of my father's death**

Unable to sleep with his silence,
she wanders through whispers
of nightshade. Horse nettles
with flowers of blue fire lie
still in the moonlight. These blooms
may quietly kill her or make her
believe she's in love—and
what is the difference?
This fistful of bullets slips
easily into the chamber
that some call a heart.
She was an oak tree
for most of her life.
Tonight, she is a dandelion
blown apart by a wish.

when I am wild with grief, the animal in me

is an antelope squirrel, small and soft, whose
nature is to bite when touched

is a wild horse that love has filled to aching
with milk, gently nudging her stillborn foal

is a bighorn sheep going weeks without water, needing
only the rain inside her, leaping from ledge—to ledge

is a hummingbird plunging into every bud of sweetness
that opens in mourning, fighting to hold herself up

is a fawn on unsteady legs standing over its mother—
hunted out of season—waiting for her to wake

is a white-throated woodrat that builds her young a
heavy house from scraps of sadness others have abandoned

is an owl that steals the head of a live chicken,
taking its memories back to her nest

is a centipede whose sorrow has one hundred legs,
sheltering for winter in the darkest corner of the room

is a long-nosed bat that feeds on the nectar of night blooming
things: like agave and dreams of those we have lost

is a Gila lizard at a funeral in shining black beads
and long, sharp claws—ready to dig

is a desert tortoise holding her heart in a quiet shell,
knowing for certain her loneliness will outlive me

Dream with mother of pearl

I want to say something about bells.
No. Bones. I meant wedding
dress. Oxeye daisies nodding,
solemn as ghosts. Yes,
I hear the mountain goats.
The little bells they wear
so I can chase them down
and have my fill of milk
or is it wool I'm wishing
for? I am no body's
betrothed, a girl with
a pearl handled knife.
I want to sing you a mission.
A lily that rings. A pale
horse with a braided mane.
A hawk tree. Crabapple
flowers and fingernail
moon. My Iroquois
grandmother asking
again and again
in a white night
gown four times
her size. Child.
Where are my hands?

Pelican

A pelican folds and unfolds
the air over the ocean like
a woman taking in her sheets.
What does it mean to live
in such grace? At the ocean,
ghosts of lovers I'd almost forgotten
come back in waves. One was
the shore I broke myself against.
One loved like a filleting knife
and yet another held me
together with nets. Tonight
while the pelican sleeps
I hear them whispering things
that are not meant for me.
They are voices roaring in a shell.
I am the unknowable silence
they drown in.

Materia prima

If I sleep with windows closed
and a bird sings but I don't hear,
            is it real?
I have never questioned
birds—the very hearts of trees.
I am asking about my life.
If I could breathe before a bee
mistook me for a blooming
thing and pierced me through.
What my hands knew before
they opened an avocado
grown in Mexico and held
its warm, unyielding seed.
Have I opened my arms to
anyone as long as the saguaros
that surround this house? I see
myself through other eyes.
To the cat, I am a branch.
To rain, a bowl. Sometimes
I forget that most of me is water.
And you: a body of water I love.
We witness one another beautiful
but we are strangers to this place.
We have not learned
the language of the whales
who speak in darkness
who testify in darkness
who sing the stillness
and the miracles, whose
lowest psalm could lull
our pulse or break our bones.
When the baleen whale
falls silent, who's to say
if we were really here at all?

Starling

Pry me open. Use a palette knife.
Or your nails, broken on burrows
you dug for the tortoise. See?
I hold a desert in my mouth.
You gave me this hare.
This ocotillo always in bloom.
The bell curve of a nude who
will never die, her white hip
a calcium that wraps around me
as I learn to pearl. Did you mean
for me to keep your starling
all this time? It has been years.
Thank you for what I know
of love's sharp beak. Its feathers,
more brilliant in winter.
The sudden and strange
murmuration of flight.
The moon on my tongue
is nearly full. It lights your face.
I never meant anything to you.

I walked a desert wanting

I walked
a desert wanting
some wild thing
to make me love again—
a Broad-winged Hawk,
a Mexican wolf, a raving
Queen of the Night.
I found nothing
but a pair of mining
bees, tiny prophets
of the coming storm.
All they had was light.
All they knew of love
was hauling life
from the bursting
hearts of marigolds,
giving it all to the
ground, and making
more.

No greater love

Thank you fire, for not taking Frankie.
For spitting him out, shiny and whole
as a watermelon seed in his family's hands.
Thank you hands that hitchhike deserts to dig
in the dirt, pick pecans, and plant olive trees.
Thank you sycamore for feeling like my father's
skin. Thank you aspen for mimicking the magic
of Mamaw's white hair. Thank you prickly
pear for feeding the mule deer and piercing
my heart. Thank you javelina lying in the middle
of the road that summer night, thank you swerving
car, thank you husband who feared you dead but
returned to find you were nursing two sucklings
on the yellow lines—thank you for knowing
the meaning of love but not of danger. Thank you
dangerous sting of the bark scorpion in my house
for pulling me out of the dark evening news.
Thank you Ukraine for refusing to yield—and for
the 20 million metric tons of potatoes you gave us.
Thank you corn for growing taller and stronger
than me. Thank you sugar beet, milk cow, and egg.
Thank you clean cotton sheets. Thank you lover
your mess and your mop of dark hair. Thank you
tomcat for living beyond your nine lives to fill our
one with wildness. Thank you bare feet in the stream.
Thank you minnow and moss. Thank you friend
who went too soon for leaving your laugh like
a photograph we can go back to. Thank you
one hundred and seven degrees for bleaching
the cholla's bones so we can touch them.
Thank you mostly cloudy day and monsoon June
instead of July. Thank you jalapeno jam with blackberries
hailing us from some hole-in-the-wall at Rock Springs.
Thank you Flagstaff for your scent of pine, soft
thunder of your running deer. Thank you Eddie's
electric guitar. Thank you Sara for swinging low
with the holy gospel of bluegrass, and thank

you Johnny Cash. Thank you ring of fire
for circling all the way back to the beginning,
when gratitude was the only music we knew.

And did we love

Wasn't it rutted?
Weren't there thorns?
We envied the desert's
indefinite light—
mesquite trees flickering
like movies in the darkness.
Aren't we fallen?
My marrow, thick
with ravens. Your wet
hair. I nearly went blind
photographing the sun
through your creosote
blooms, their resin smelling
of fresh rain, roots killing
all that grew close.
Can a life be rewilded?
Strangers to grace,
we built our house
on a fox den.
Pulled packrat nests
from our engines.
Fed the birds at first
but soon forgot. And
did we love? God
asks again. His eye
is on the sparrow.
We are little thistles
in his heart.

Stacey Forbes won first place in the *2021 Plough Poetry Prize*, and was a semi-finalist for the 2023 Adrienne Rich Award for Poetry. Her poems are published or forthcoming in *Atlanta Review, Beloit Poetry Journal, Crab Creek Review, New Ohio Review, and Terrain*, among others. Born in the Pennsylvania countryside, Stacey now lives in Tucson, Arizona.

www.ingramcontent.com/pod-product-compliance
Lightning Source LLC
Chambersburg PA
CBHW022102080426
42734CB00009B/1459